JAMES MADISON
Founder and President
BY TAMARA ORR STAATS

Boston, Massachusetts
Chandler, Arizona
Glenview, Illinois
Upper Saddle River, New Jersey

Illustrations
2 (T), 9, 10, 11, 12 Len Ebert.

Photographs
Every effort has been made to secure permission and provide appropriate credit for photographic material.
The publisher deeply regrets any omission and pledges to correct errors called to its attention in subsequent editions.

Unless otherwise acknowledged, all photographs are the property of Pearson Education, Inc.

Photo locators denoted as follows: Top (T), Center (C), Bottom (B), Left (L), Right (R), Background (Bkgd)

Opener: Prints & Photographs Division, LC-DIG-ppmsca-30581/Library of Congress; 1 Prints & Photographs Division, LC-DIG-ppmsca-30581/Library of Congress; 2 (B) Thinkstock; 4 Prints & Photographs Division, LC-USZC4-1583/Library of Congress; 5 Prints & Photographs Division, LC-DIG-pga-03359/Library of Congress; 6 Prints & Photographs Division, LC-DIG-ppmsca-05483/Library of Congress; 7 Theodor Horydczak Collection, Prints & Photographs Division, LC-H8-CT-V05-002/Library of Congress; 8 Prints & Photographs Division, LC-USZC4-9904/Library of Congress; 13 Photolibrary Group, Inc.; 14 Prints & Photographs Division, LC-USZ62-68175/Library of Congress; 15 Prints & Photographs Division, LC-DIG-ppmsca-30581/Library of Congress.

ISBN-13: 978-0-328-67633-0
ISBN-10: 0-328-67633-0

10 16

Little Jemmy

When James Madison was a boy, he was small for his age. His father called him "Little Jemmy." He had a soft voice, and he was often sick. He sometimes had spells. His body would stiffen, and he would fall down and black out for a few minutes. Even when grown, he did not have a tall or strong body.

James Madison was the country's fourth president.

However, Madison did have a strong mind, and he did become a strong leader. He became the fourth president of the United States. And he was one of the **founders** of our country. His ideas helped shape the government we have today.

Growing Up

James Madison was born on March 16, 1751, in the **colony** of Virginia. Madison grew up on a large farm with a view of the Blue Ridge Mountains. His father raised tobacco, and the family was wealthy.

Because young Madison was often sick, he spent a lot of time indoors. He was taught at home by his mother and grandmother. Madison was curious and always asking questions, and he loved to read. By the time he was 11 years old, he had read every one of the 85 books in his father's library.

Blue Ridge Mountains

Education

When Madison was 11, his father sent him off to boarding school, a school where students live as well as study. His teacher, Donald Robertson, taught his students to ask questions and to think clearly. He taught them French, Greek, and Latin, as well as history and mathematics.

When he was 16, Madison's father called him home. Now he had a private teacher to prepare him for college.

At home, much of the talk was about **taxes**. Many Virginians, including Madison's father, were not happy with the new taxes Great Britain was making the colonies pay.

Colonists showed their anger about the new British taxes.

The College of New Jersey

In 1769 Madison left Virginia and rode off on his horse to attend the College of New Jersey. This college is now known as Princeton University. Madison was shy, but he made many friends there.

It was an exciting time to be at college. Everyone was talking about what was going on in the country. People everywhere seemed to be angry about British taxes. Madison and the other students approved when merchants stopped buying goods from Britain.

At college, Madison read many more books and thought about things like government, power, and freedom. He worked very hard and did well. He finished college in two years and then went home to Virginia.

Revolution

More and more, the talk in the country was about the British taxes. People were starting to prepare for a war to gain **independence**.

Madison and his father were appointed to a local group. Their job was to make sure that if war came, the people were ready. Madison trained with the local **militia**. He was proud that he was a very good shot.

Then in April 1775, fighting broke out between the colonists and British soldiers in Lexington, Massachusetts. The American **Revolution** had begun.

Colonists fought British soldiers at Lexington.

Madison and other leaders worked in the capitol in Williamsburg, Virginia.

Working for Virginia

In 1776 leaders from all the colonies were meeting in Philadelphia at the Continental Congress. On July 4 they approved the Declaration of Independence, declaring the colonies to be free of British rule.

Meantime, the colonies—now called states— needed new governments. Madison was chosen to help write Virginia's new **constitution**. He had very strong opinions, especially on the right to worship freely. The government, he thought, should not try to tell people what to believe. So he made sure that Virginia's constitution protected freedom of religion.

Late in 1777, Madison was elected to the eight-man governor's **council**. One exciting part of this job was that Madison worked closely with Thomas Jefferson. It was Jefferson who had written the Declaration of Independence just the year before. The two men found they worked well together and had a lot in common. They both loved to read, and collected books. Both loved science and history. Madison and Jefferson became lifelong friends.

Thomas Jefferson (right) worked with Benjamin Franklin (left) and John Adams (center) on the Declaration of Independence.

A Weak Plan

In 1780, Madison was chosen to be a **delegate** to the Continental Congress in Philadelphia. One of the jobs of the Congress was to plan a government for the new country. Madison attended the meetings and listened. Many of the leaders were afraid of a strong central government. After all, they were fighting to be free of the British king.

So the delegates designed a government that gave most of the power to the states. The national government had the power to make war, but not much else. This first constitution was called the Articles of Confederation. Madison didn't think it would work very well.

Under the Articles of Confederation, each state printed its own money.

The British surrender

Finally, in 1783, the war was over. Americans had won their independence!

But Madison was worried. He had studied history and government for many years. He was sure that the Articles of Confederation were too weak. It wasn't long before Madison was proved right. People could see the government wasn't working.

Madison had been thinking for a while about a better plan of government. He read all he could about kinds of governments. His friend Thomas Jefferson, who was now in France, sent him a trunk load of books. Madison read them, too.

A New Plan

In 1787, fifty-five of America's leaders met in Philadelphia. They were there to make the Articles of Confederation stronger. The delegates included Madison, Benjamin Franklin, and others. George Washington was put in charge of the meeting. Many of the delegates had helped write the constitutions for their own states.

Madison was at every meeting. Every day he took detailed notes. Thanks to him we have a very good idea of what happened.

George Washington speaks to delegates at the meeting.

Three Branches of Government

Executive	Legislative	Judicial
		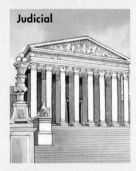

Under the United States Constitution, the three branches of government share power.

The delegates were supposed to fix the Articles of Confederation. But Madison didn't think the Articles could be fixed. He had a better idea—a new plan. He and the other leaders from Virginia called it the "Virginia Plan."

The Virginia Plan called for a strong central government with three branches. Each branch would make sure the others did not become too powerful. Each branch worked as a check on the power of the others.

All summer long the delegates argued about the plan. When they disagreed, they made **compromises**. Little by little they worked out their differences. Finally, in September, the delegates agreed on a plan. Most of Madison's ideas were in it. Now the states had to agree, too.

The Bill of Rights

The Constitution needed nine states to approve it. But people in several states refused to approve. There was no list of rights, they said.

So Madison wrote a set of **amendments**, or changes, to the Constitution. These first ten amendments became known as the Bill of Rights. Now there was a written promise that Americans would have freedom of speech, religion, the press, and other rights. By 1790, all 13 states had approved the Constitution. Madison's plan for government was now law.

Freedom of the press means newspapers can write about any topic.

Dolley Madison

On September 15, 1794, Madison surprised many people. He got married. Dolley Madison was very outgoing and charming. She was very smart, too. She knew a lot about government and what was going on in the country.

When James Madison became the country's fourth president in 1809, Dolley Madison entertained people at the White House. She became well known for her weekly gatherings. Sometimes she served a new frozen dessert from France, called ice cream.

President Madison

When Madison became president, France and Britain had been fighting with one another for a long time. The United States traded goods with both countries and was caught in the middle of their disagreement. By 1812, the United States was drawn into the war on the side of the French.

In 1814 British troops entered Washington, D.C., and set fire to much of the city. Madison barely escaped. The war ended with a peace agreement late in 1814.

When his time as president ended, Madison returned to his home in Virginia. Today he is remembered for the huge part he played in designing our government. He is known as the "Father of the Constitution."

Glossary

amendment a change or addition to the Constitution

colony a place ruled by another country

compromise the settling of a disagreement by each side giving up part of what it wants

constitution a written plan for government

council a group of advisors

delegate someone who represents, or speaks for, a larger group of people

founder a person who starts or builds something

independence freedom from another country's rule

militia a group of ordinary citizens who fought in times of emergency during the American Revolution

revolution a war fought to replace one government with another one

tax money paid to a government

JAMES MADISON

Founder and President

BY TAMARA ORR STAATS

Boston, Massachusetts
Chandler, Arizona
Glenview, Illinois
Upper Saddle River, New Jersey

Illustrations
2 (T), 9, 10, 11, 12 Len Ebert.

Photographs
Every effort has been made to secure permission and provide appropriate credit for photographic material.
The publisher deeply regrets any omission and pledges to correct errors called to its attention in subsequent editions.

Unless otherwise acknowledged, all photographs are the property of Pearson Education, Inc.

Photo locators denoted as follows: Top (T), Center (C), Bottom (B), Left (L), Right (R), Background (Bkgd)

Opener: Prints & Photographs Division, LC-DIG-ppmsca-30581/Library of Congress; 1 Prints & Photographs Division, LC-DIG-ppmsca-30581/Library of Congress; 2 (B) Thinkstock; 4 Prints & Photographs Division, LC-USZC4-1583/Library of Congress; 5 Prints & Photographs Division, LC-DIG-pga-03359/Library of Congress; 6 Prints & Photographs Division, LC-DIG-ppmsca-05483/Library of Congress; 7 Theodor Horydczak Collection, Prints & Photographs Division, LC-H8-CT-V05-002/Library of Congress; 8 Prints & Photographs Division, LC-USZC4-9904/Library of Congress; 13 Photolibrary Group, Inc.; 14 Prints & Photographs Division, LC-USZ62-68175/Library of Congress; 15 Prints & Photographs Division, LC-DIG-ppmsca-30581/Library of Congress.

ISBN-13: 978-0-328-67633-0
ISBN-10:   0-328-67633-0

10   16